MW01533699

Is God Freedom?

Michael John DeNucci

Second Edition
December 2023
Printed in the United States
By http://thebookpatch.com
ISBN 9798890902887

First Edition December 2021

Dedication

I dedicate this book to my loving wife for 34 years, Kathy, who passed away almost six years ago and is now my soulmate for eternity. Kathy, thank you for giving me your heart as my wife, which helped inspire my books. You taught me so much about love which I shall never forget.

Acknowledgements

First and foremost, I thank God, Who, through the Holy Spirit, inspired me to write this book. My gratitude to God is overwhelming!

Also, I thank my siblings and friends for supporting me in writing this book. In particular, I thank my brother Donald for formatting and facilitating the printing of this book.

Table of Contents

Preface

I believe that God is Freedom. His Commandments of Love of Him and neighbor as ourselves remove restrictions in our lives due to sin. When free of sin, we maintain a healthy relationship with God and others and experience happiness. When we sin, we close off the relationship with God, not because He rejects us, but because we reject Him. But, God always offers us forgiveness to reconcile with Him to find Freedom to do good, with all the rewards of doing so. God truly is Freedom. That is the case I will build in this book.

Introduction

"This is my prayer to you, O Lord! Give to me your special favor. Pour out your truth and mercy on me in an abundance, that will enable me to put your love into practice, filling me with true affection for You and my neighbor."

St. Vincent de Paul

1
Our Plans and God's Plans

Our plans can fail to be executed or simply "fold up". However, God's plans always unfold just the way He wants them to unfold.

To find happiness in life, we must make our plans in line with God's plans by following his words in Scripture, religious writings and other real-life sources, as influenced by the Holy Spirit. Then, we will find that God's plan for us is happiness—the Truth, for God is Happiness and the Truth!

2
My Need for God

Without God, I lack meaning and direction in life. My direction in my life comes from the Holy Spirit, particularly in writing my books.

Without God, I think I would suffer from a feeling of hopelessness with no meaning in life. God grants me His love, which gives me hope and direction. God reveals His truths to me through the Holy Spirit. God is the Truth!

3
What is Relationship?

Relationship is simply relating to someone—not necessarily in a close intimate fashion, which is implied by the word "relationship". It does not have to include "intimacy" with all the commitment involved in an exclusive relationship. Indeed, we all have relationships with persons with whom we relate. Thus, we are commanded by Jesus to love everyone as best we can and respect their needs for love.

4
Stewards of our Lives

We are entrusted by God with our lives, Who puts us "in charge" of our lives as stewards of them. Our lives are actually the property of God. But, He gives us freedom to make decisions to serve Him, others and ourselves in that stewardship.

5
Jesus: Accused of Blasphemy

Jesus was crucified because He threatened the power and influence of the religious leaders at that time— particularly the Jewish High Priest Caiaphas. They stated that Jesus deserved death because He claimed to be the Son of God, which was blasphemy according to their Jewish law. Of course, Jesus spoke the Truth when claiming to be the Son of God.

However, I believe that their reason to crucify Jesus was just an excuse to try to legitimize it.

The real reason was because Jesus had gained so much popularity and influence with the masses of people at that time, that those leaders feared Him and were jealous of His influence because He threatened their own power and influence over the people.

6
Timing in My Life

After mentioning "timing" in my first book, "Thoughts and Writings", I am again finding "timing" in my life. What I am thinking about matches the words of a song to which I am listening.

A deacon visiting our church once said he had "coincidences" in his life, which I now consider timing. For example the license plate on the car in front of him read "deacon" when driving. Then, his stop on his trip read "Deacon" on the mailbox. That happened after he had turned down requests from persons in his church that he become a deacon. Overwhelmed by the "coincidences" or "timing", he did become a deacon.

Timing occurred this time with me in that as I was proof reading my last book, I read "The Rivers of Babylon" in the table of contents, just as the song "The Rivers of Babylon" was playing on my phone. I did NOT plan that. It just happened. Then, just after hearing that song, the song "Good Timing" played. These "coincidences" I attribute to the Holy Spirit to give order to my life and help my life make more sense and give me direction.

7
Does God Restrict our Freedom?

Too many people think that God restricts or inhibits their freedom. But, that is not the case.

By surrendering to God, we remove doubt and fear from our lives through trust in Him. God's commandments to love increase our freedom rather than restrict it. By loving God and others, we remove the idea and/or feeling that others, including God, could be our enemies rather than our friends.

God wants our friendship and for us to have friendships with others. He is a positive force in our lives, which increases our freedom from worry, addictions and prejudices. God is Love, Happiness and Freedom!

8
Love Covers Many Sins

The following is a quote from "Quiet Moments with Padre Pio" by Patricia Treece, p. 81:

"Many Sins are forgiven thee. Have you not for some time loved the Lord? Do you not Love Him now? Do you not love Him forever? Therefore, do not fear! Even conceded that you have committed all the sins in the world, Jesus repeats to you: Many sins are forgiven thee because thou hast loved much!"

9
Prayer: Do we Enjoy it?

I have said that prayer should be enjoyable. It is communicating with our best friend—God. If prayer is not enjoyable, we might be doing it wrong. Are we simply repeating prayers that are someone else's words rather than our own?

If so, perhaps we should try to pray from the "heart"—what we really feel and believe. Then, maybe, if we pray in our own words, we will feel more natural and sincere, rather than like a robot going through the motions, with little emotional satisfaction. Prayer should be enjoyable—even prayer of repentance to God, because it helps remove the guilt by admitting it to God, knowing that He forgives us.

Finally, prayer is an act of love expressed to God, which can give us Freedom from worry and fear. Prayer to God is Freedom.

"Prayer is the best weapon we have. It is the key to God's heart. You must speak to Jesus, not only with your lips, but with your heart; in fact on certain occasions.... only with your heart."

From "Quiet Moments with Padre Pio" by Patricia Treece, p. 86.

The song on my phone just played "Love Put a Song in My HEART", again indicating timing in my life.

10
Surrendering to God: Freedom

After surrendering to the Allies (including the U.S.A) in World War Two, West Germany did not succumb to slavery, but probably enjoyed more freedom than its citizens did under Hitler. I believe our democratic values transferred more freedom to West Germany back then and to Germany today, since East Germany gained freedom from the Soviet Union.

So it is with God, even more so. By surrendering to God, we increase, not decrease our freedom, because we are more free of slavery due to sin and fear. God is truly Freedom!

11
Are Guilt and Fear Related?

Yes. Fear often comes from guilt—the fear that we will be punished after doing something wrong, thus, from guilt. However, if we are too scrupulous or bound to some irrational doctrine, we may suffer guilt and fear where neither is due. Do we feel guilty for transgressing some important Law of God or society, or is our guilt and fear based on superstition or ignorance?

We should look to the 10 commandments which Jesus condensed into two: Love God with all your heart, mind, soul and strength, and love your neighbor or as yourself. Also, did we disobey some just law of society? If we are OK with God's laws and society's just laws, perhaps we should not feel so guilty to cause us to fear punishment. And, of course, we should not feel guilty for any 'forgiven" offenses.

God is Love, Happiness, Truth and Freedom.

12
What is Spirituality?

Spirituality is a concept meaning not necessarily being tied to any religious sect or organization, but transcending that. It is having a sense of trying to become Godly or Godlike, but NOT trying to become God. It requires humility and we can do it by practicing virtues, especially the virtue of Love. The more we become Godly or Godlike, the more perfected our spirit. From this attempt at "spiritual perfection" comes more Freedom because we can be more free of worry and sin. God is Freedom.

13
Is God Patient?

Yes, indeed, God is patient. He never tires of loving us. Even when we sin, He offers us forgiveness. Even the worst sinner can be forgiven.

Consider St. Paul, known as Saul before his conversion to become a bold advocate for Jesus after Jesus patiently asked him "Saul, Saul, why do you persecute me?" Saul had approved the persecution of the early Christians, including the first Christian martyr, St. Stephen. In his own words, he confessed: "I persecuted this Way to death, binding both men and women and delivering them to prison." Acts 9: 2,4

There is no limit to God's patience as exemplified by his forgiveness of all who repent. God is Patient! God is Freedom!

14
Understanding a Person's Motives

Understanding is a "gift" of the Holy Spirit, from which we can learn of another's motives. It is sometimes proper to try to learn of another's motives, especially if we do it in an honest and forgiving manner.

Motives can be "good" or "bad". However, it is often difficult to discern a person's motives, but it is not necessarily impossible.

Understanding another's motives can actually lead us to forgive them, but not necessarily condone their behavior, if it was wrong. When we forgive others, we free ourselves from bitterness towards them, and possibly even towards life itself.

Finally, if we forgive others, God can then forgive us when we sin. Consider The Lords's Prayer: "Forgive us our trespasses AS WE FORGIVE THOSE WHO TRESPASS AGAINST US". Forgiveness offers us freedom from bitterness towards others and towards life itself. God is Freedom!

15
Fear of the Lord: Losing God's Love

This "gift of the Holy Spirit" does not mean only fearing God due to His punishment if we offend Him, but fearing loss of His love if we reject His love and are separated from Him by sinning. We cannot be truly happy without God's love.

God's love is free; God is Freedom by moving us away from bondage due to sin and towards virtue, so that we are under His protection from His Love.

16
The Danger in Believing We have Almost Unlimited Freedom

Some people think that they have almost unlimited freedom—that they can do almost anything they want. However, this notion of almost unlimited freedom can result in LIMITING their freedom. We cannot do whatever we want, but are, of course, bound by the laws of society and, most importantly, the laws of God, which often are the source of society's laws. If we disobey these laws, we will probably, if not certainly, suffer loss of freedom.

In conclusion, what may seem like limiting freedom by obeying laws, may result in maintaining or even INCREASING freedom. God is Freedom!

17
Jesus Christ: Humility, Love and Obedience

Jesus was humble in spite of the fear he faced when arrested. At that time, He said: "So, if you are looking for me, let these men go" (referring to His apostles). Then, Simon Peter, who had a sword and drew it, struck the High Priest's slave and cut off his right ear...Jesus said to Peter: "Put your sword into its scabbard. Shall I not drink the cup that the Father gave me?" John. 18:8-11. Jesus was obedient to His Father. "Then Jesus touched the servant's ear and healed it." Luke 22:51

Jesus could probably could have raised an insurrection to defend Himself, if He and His followers had planned it earlier. Peter thought he might defend Him even when the arrest was imminent.

However, Jesus knew His fate and did not want an insurrection, but offered Himself as example to all mankind, perhaps, of the greatest love man has ever known by laying down His life for us to show us the way.

Pilate asked Jesus: "Are you king of the Jews?" John: 18:33 Jesus answered: "My kingdom does not belong to this world; My attendants would be fighting to keep me from being handed over to the Jews. But, as it is, my kingdom is not here". John 18: 35-36.

So, Jesus was and still is "savior" on a spiritual level, but not on a political level. He brought salvation and freedom to us by "testifying to the truth" as the "Way, the Truth and the Life". He courageously met fear with love, rather than hate, to show us that God is Love and the Truth.

18
How Could God's Commandments be Freedom?

The Commandments of Jesus are of Love: Love of God and Love of Neighbor as Ourselves. Rather than restrict our freedom, these commandments increase our freedom.

Love is a liberating activity. Notice I say activity—not just a concept. Also, Love is an "act of the will", not just a feeling, though feelings may be important in Love.

Love was meant by Jesus to liberate us from the bondage of sin. Practicing Love has so many beneficial effects or results for both the giver and receiver. Acts of charity based on Love can improve the lives of people, whether it be in gifts of money or material goods, or simply kind words or good deeds. Also, giving Love can bring the "giver" Joy. Love truly does "make the world go around".

Just as Love is Freedom, God is Freedom to liberate us for Happiness in this lifetime and/or the afterlife.

19
Jesus is Powerful

Consider all the miracles that Jesus performed during His life as a human on earth: curing the sick, healing the blind and disabled, and even raising the dead (Lazarus).

Jesus was and still is the Son of God. He received and still receives his power from His Father, who raised Him from the dead to prove the power of God. Jesus is the most powerful human to ever exist, being Divine Himself —being both wholly human and wholly God.

Finally, He offers us a "way out from sin"—forgiveness and everlasting life. Jesus gave Himself as an example to emulate in our lives to lead us to Freedom and Everlasting Happiness. Just as He is Freedom, God is Freedom.

20
The Trinity and Freedom

The Trinity is defined as three persons in one God. Jesus referred to His Father, God the Father, and to His Spirit, the Holy Spirit, Whom He would send to His apostles on Pentecost after His death, resurrection and ascension into heaven, to inspire them to overcome their fears and boldly advocate for Him, beginning the spread of Christianity.

Jesus was and is God to Humanity—superior to us. The Trinity is a simple and good way to teach us about God and our relationship to Him, but it is a mystery. God is Freedom, for when we know the Truth, the Truth sets us Free.

21
Timing Again in My Life

One evening I had another experience of "timing" in my life. As I was reviewing my book, "Happiness is the Truth", I came to the article, "By the Rivers of Babylon", just as the song with that title was playing on U Tube on my phone. This was the second time that the playing of that song coincided with my reading. Once again, I did not plan that occurrence. It just happened.

Such timing gives me direction to believe that I am on the right path in my life, moved along by the Holy Spirit, Who is my Freedom.

22
Should We Have "Hell" on Our "Radar Screen" as We Go through Life?

No! I do not believe that we should fixate on Hell or even have it on our "radar screen" as we go through life. We should have our "sights" set on Heaven.

When driving a car, do we want to visualize accidents as we drive? Probably not, but should visualize a safe trip ending by safely reaching our destination.

So, it should be the same with life. Our final destination should be Heaven, visualizing no sins to divert us to Hell. If we focus on Heaven with God in mind, we should feel "free" that we will reach Heaven.

None of this is to say that we should not be alert for possible "dangers" to our souls—temptations to sin. However, we should feel "free" enough to enjoy our life—our trip—to reach our final destination—Heaven. God is Freedom!

23
Did Jesus Make Forgiveness of Sins Possible?

Jesus did NOT make Forgiveness of sins possible for the first time. I believe people could be forgiven of sin even before the time of Jesus.

Psalm 25: 6-7, 11 in the Old Testament (before Jesus lived on earth) states in the "Confident Prayer for Forgiveness and Guidance: "Remember your compassion and your mercy, O Lord for they are ages old. Remember, no more the sins of my youth; remember me according to your mercy, because of your goodness, Lord....For the sake of your name, Lord, pardon my guilt, though it is great."

What Jesus did was show us the Way to forgive others as God forgives us. The Lord's Prayer states: "forgive us our trespasses as we forgive those who trespass against us". These words are directly from Jesus when He tells us how to pray to our Heavenly Father.

Jesus forgave Mary Magdalene after the religious leaders walked away while preparing to stone her to death for adultery. Jesus said to those religious leaders: "Let he who is without sin cast the first stone". All those ready to stone her walked away after those words from Jesus.

Then, Jesus said to Mary Magdalene: "Who has condemned you?" She replied: "No one" for they all walked away. He said to her: "Neither will I condemn you. Go in peace and sin no more." This set the stage for future religious confession.

The Death and Resurrection of Jesus did NOT make forgiveness of sin possible for the first time, but exemplified perfect forgiveness. Also, humility is required to be forgiven of sin. He said to the thief being crucified with Him: "This day you will be with me in paradise". He forgave the thief because ~~the~~ he was humble and repentant and wanted Jesus to remember

Him in His Kingdom. Jesus forgives him of his sins and promised him Heaven.

Jesus made forgiveness of sin more important than ever before. The Old Testament read: "An eye for an eye, and a tooth for a tooth", when referring to a belief in justice before the time of Christ. Jesus proposed forgiveness instead of strict justice. Even while dying on the cross, Jesus said to those crucifying Him: "Forgive them, for they know not what they do". Again, He offered us a perfect example of "forgiveness".

Finally, forgiveness frees us of our sins and should bring us to forgive others who have offended us, thus removing any "bitterness" towards others and/or towards life itself. Forgiveness brings us Freedom. God is Freedom!

24
Does Being Free from God Bring Us Freedom?

If we surrender to God, we are free of the bondage of sin. However, if after surrendering to God, we fight to break free from God, we may find that being free from God delivers us back into slavery due to sin. We must surrender to God and never try to reject Him. However, if we do try to reject Him, He does not give up on us, but offers us forgiveness to be reconciled with Him so that we can again enjoy the Happiness based on the freedom He offers Us—Freedom from sin and worry. God truly is Freedom.

25
Using My Talent: Music

Jesus told us to not bury our talents, but use them. The story from the Bible comes to mind about the lazy servant, whom, when asked what he had done with the gifts (talents) entrusted with him, he said that he feared His master, so He buried his "talents" so that they would be safe when His master asked for them back. He admonished that lazy and fearful servant for not "investing" or using his talents to give back to his master more than received from him.

Our talents are meant for us to use for the greater glory of God and to help others. We have the Freedom to do so and should not fear using our talents for fear what others may think of us for doing so. And, never fear that God will disapprove of using our talents.

I had my first thought of using my talent of music when I decided to sing at the local nursing home. I did perform three shows there, which I believe were enjoyed by the residents and most of those whom I had invited. God and the activity director of the nursing home gave me the Freedom to do so, and I thank them for doing so. It was so enjoyable for me to sing. God is Freedom!

26
Using My Talent: Writing

Then, I started writing. First, it was just text messages to my siblings. Though I wanted to write a book, I had no concrete plan to write or publish a book at that time. Then, by copying those text messages, my brother presented me with my first book: "Thoughts and Writings" as a surprise, acting as the "publisher" himself. I was so grateful and pleased with the book that I decided go forward with his plan for "publishing" more books. To date, I have written 7 books, including this one.

After receiving compliments on my books from my family and others that I had a talent to write, I have continued writing books to use that talent. I thank God and my brother for the freedom to do so. God is Freedom!

27
Using My Talent: Caring for Children

When considering talents, I did not consider that caring for children was using a God given talent. However, while growing up in a big family —12 children- I was frequently required to care for the younger siblings, being the third oldest myself.

Now, I realize that caring for children was using a talent. Much later, after marrying, my wife and I were physically unable to have children of our own. However, we frequently took care of children of various ages—infancy through about 12 years old.

In particular, I remember caring for a toddler in Utah for my nephew and niece. One evening the toddler was crying uncontrollably, so I put her on my lap and sang the song "If I Fell" by the Beatles to her. We looked into each other's eyes and she stopped crying and said the word "eyes", probably a word she had recently learned. I believe my singing to her was using a talent. I believe that I have used other talents when caring for children, including dancing.

I realize now that I have used talents that I did not know I even had, and I thank God for giving me the Freedom to use those talents. God truly is Freedom!

28
Forgiveness vs. Judgment

At times we may feel that we have been cheated or offended by others. We have two roads which we could follow after such an event.

One, we could judge them and condemn them based on hatred or fear of them hurting us again and cut off the relationship.

Or, two, we could forgive them and move forward with our relationship with them, if they want it, considering that the "offense" could have been unintentional or just a misunderstanding.

None of this is to say that we cannot defend ourselves, but should be careful of judging others. Christ said: "Woe to you who judge, lest you be judged". He also said: "If someone strikes you on the cheek, turn to him the other cheek". If we return LOVE after being offended, it can sometimes win the other persons over, because they may not know how to respond to such love except by accepting us. Lover conquers all and gives us Freedom—Freedom from bitterness towards others who we feel have offended us. As Love is Freedom, God is Freedom!

29
Does God Need Our Love?

Yes. I believe that God needs our love as a close friend needs our love. He knows us better than we know ourselves.

God is a "being" like us rather than just "energy". He is not "above" having needs and needs our friendship. He wants to help us navigate through this life until we are literally with Him in Heaven. God offers us Freedom from anything that distracts us from Him, like sin. If we surrender to His Love, He will rejoice because He needs our Love.

God truly is Freedom, because He is Love, the Truth and Happiness!

30
The Origin of Mankind

I have a theory of the origin of mankind not directly based on Scripture or science. Could it be that the first man and woman were placed here on Earth from another planet? That planet could be what we call Heaven, where God reigns with the saints and angels. (See my book- Fishing for Heaven, article 1.)

This theory is more in line with the Genesis version of creation in the Bible than evolution. (See my book-Is God Happiness? article 10.). This theory states that the first man and woman were placed here by God and given rules to follow in the new environment, which they disobeyed, resulting in a more difficult life than they had at first in the "Garden of Eden". This disobedience and resulting suffering could be referred to as "the fall of man" as indicated in the Bible.

31
The Christmas Star

The Christmas Star as explained in the Bible led the "wise men" to Bethlehem, then stopped over the stable where Jesus lay. However, stars do not appear to move in the sky, so how could that "star" lead the wise men to Jesus, moving and then stopping over the stable in Bethlehem?

I propose that the Christmas Star was NOT a star at all, but a type of "spacecraft" from another planet (Heaven) from where the Holy Spirit had blessed Mary to conceive of Jesus. That "spacecraft" could certainly move in the sky until stopping over the stable in Bethlehem.

I do not believe a completely literal interpretation of the Bible is necessary to receive the message from Scripture. God gives us the freedom to reason in searching for the Truth. God is Freedom.

32
Visualizing our Future

We can visualize something that we want to happen in our future. Then, we can make a sound plan and execute it to obtain the outcome we desire. Thus, we can "make our future", but ONLY if God allows it to occur. Simply visualizing our future does not make it happen.

We can visualize achieving something sinful— something not in God's plan. Sinful events do occur, but only because we have free will to cause them to occur by committing sin.

Wise plans can bring about virtuous acts or desirable events, according to God's plan. God grants us the Freedom to make wise plans and, then execute them for Good results. God is Freedom.

33
Are the Rules Good?

Our society, including our formal religions, have "rules" to follow intended to help lead us to a   peaceful, prosperous and happy life.

But, do the rules actually do that or do they not fit the current times? The Old Testament rule of "an eye for an eye and a tooth for a tooth" is an outdated rule which is an expression of strict justice based on revenge rather than love and forgiveness, as taught by Jesus.

We have the ability to reason to decide if a rule is "just" in current times. However, we must realize that breaking certain rules, even if they seem "unjust", may lead to undesirable consequences for us and/or others. We should always consider consequences of our actions.

In conclusion, are the rules consistent with the Ten Commandments condensed into the two commandments of Love that Jesus gave us? If so, they are probably good rules, if practical. God gives each of us the Freedom to decide. Always, decide on the side of Goodness based on the Truth. God is Truth and Freedom.

34
Doing the Right Thing

We may do things that seem advantageous to us. We may gain a lot of money, power, and prestige or obtain other benefits from doing things. But, are our actions the "right thing to do"? Are they what God expects of us? Or are they simply based on selfish desires meant to help only ourselves or, worse yet, to harm others for our own benefit?

God offers us Freedom to do the "right thing". We will never be satisfied with lasting Happiness unless we do so. God is Freedom.

35
Do We Pass the Test of Love for God?

Life brings to us difficult situations which can be interpreted as a "test of our Love for God". Look to Job in the Old Testament. Even with serious misfortunes, he kept his faith in God, so he passed the test and obtained the reward of more material goods than he had before the misfortunes.

Covid19 could be such a test for us today due to all the threats of illness, death, and the inconvenience due to precautions to mitigate the spread of the disease. Some of us have actually experienced serious illness or deaths of loved ones ourselves due to Covid19.

We "pass the test" if we maintain our faith and trust in God and our Love for God during these trials. Other illnesses, such as cancer, also can put us to the "test". If we do "pass the test", God will reward us, if not in this lifetime, then in the next lifetime.

36
Was Christ's Death the Will of His Father?

Yes. However, Jesus did not die as a "ransom" for our sins. God did not blackmail mankind into having Jesus die as a "ransom" for receiving forgiveness of our sins.

Jesus died so that we would know the Truth—that the resurrection and afterlife was real. If

Jesus had not died; He could not have been resurrected by His Father. He proved that Everlasting Life is possible for us though His Resurrection.

Jesus died due to the sins of those responsible for crucifying Him. Primarily, it was Judas, who probably was not aware that Jesus would be crucified when betraying Him, and the Jewish leaders and their followers. Those Jewish leaders and their followers wanted Him crucified at that time. As for Pilate and the Roman soldiers, and possibly even those Jews involved with crucifying Him, Jesus said: "Forgive them, so they know not what they do".

In conclusion, some wrongly view Christ's death as a "business decision" by God—that mankind had a debt to pay to God which was paid off by the death of Christ. Also, concerning ourselves, today, I do not view it that way. If we repent, there is no debt to pay for sin. God offers us forgiveness as a free gift, if we repent of our sins and are truly sorry for them. God is Freedom!

37
Jesus: His Kingdom on Earth

I believe that some people think that with Jesus's "second coming" that He will establish His "political" kingdom on earth. I doubt that He will do that.

When asked by Pilate whether he was King of the Jews, Jesus answered: "My kingdom is not of this world".

When Jesus has His second coming, we do not know what it will be like. He said that He will come like a "thief in the night"—unexpectedly. However, if the "kingdom of God" is within us, we have nothing to fear and we can meet Him in a welcoming rather than a fearful manner, if we are still living then.

In conclusion, Christ's "Kingdom within us" is already here among all his followers. We should not fear the "end of the world" when He might come, because if we are His faithful followers, we can know that we are ready for Him even if we suffer or die in some terrible tribulation, if we are living at that time. Like the thief on the cross, Christ will remember us in His Kingdom.

38
Know the Truth and it will Set You Free

When faced with an uncomfortable memory, do we try to forget it or face it head on to resolve the conflict it causes within us? Too often, I think we do the former.

Psychiatry uses drugs and procedures such as "shock treatment" to help patients forget "bad memories", which are often considered to be the cause of depression or other forms of mental illness. "Shock treatment" and some drugs probably tend to have that effect. Sometimes, such treatment is warranted. Drugs or procedures may help one get through a psychiatric emergency or even help maintain mental health. They have a place.

However, instead of doing things to forget bad memories, I propose that we try to resolve the internal conflicts they cause. I have resolved the conflicts caused by bad memories within me. By doing so, I have been set free, because I know the Truth and do not simply avoid the truth by trying to forget it. "Know the truth and the truth will set you free." (from Scripture)

In conclusion, I do not recommend anything specifically against psychiatric treatment or advice. I simply recommend that we face our bad memories instead of trying to forget them, if we believe we can resolve the conflicts they create within us. If we face them, we may find we can know the truth and it will set us free. If we find that we have done wrong based on those memories, we can ask for forgiveness from God, and if possible, from those we may have offended. Also, regrets can bring us to not repeating mistakes. On the other hand, if someone has offended us, we can forgive them and remove all bitterness related to those bad memories. Then, we are truly set Free. God is truly Freedom.

39
Is it Better to Aim High and Miss or to Aim Low and Hit?

The question above is interesting to me. I believe it is better to aim high and miss than to aim low and hit. However, we should set goals for ourselves that are reasonably attainable. If we do not, we may be setting ourselves up for disappointment.

On the other hand, we should not arbitrarily set limits on what we can achieve. If we trust God rather than relying only on our own efforts, or "rely on divine assistance" as Padre Pio stated, we may be able to reach high goals rather than settling for mediocre achievement. The key is to trust God. (Through the Year with Padre Pio by Patricia Treece) When we fail to achieve our goals, it could be that we have relied too much on ourselves instead of divine assistance, according to Padre Pio. The key is to trust God, Who is Love, Happiness, Truth and Freedom.

40
Before Jesus, Who was the "Gatekeeper" to Heaven?

I have said repeatedly in my books that Jesus is the "gatekeeper" Whom we will meet after our earthly deaths, who will judge us to let us enter Heaven or be denied entrance. Scripture supports this statement.

But, what about those Holy people before Jesus (from the Old Testament)? What about Abraham, Moses and many more, like the prophets, at least some of whom I would consider Saints? I cannot believe that they did not enter Heaven after dying. Perhaps, they met Yahweh, who was God, as manifested to Moses by the "burning bush" in the Old Testament. Ex 3:14-15.

In conclusion, I believe some persons before Jesus's time entered Heaven. Jesus offered "everlasting life". However, some Jews did believe in the Resurrection of the Dead, but evidence of that I found to be scanty in Scripture. Ez 37: 1-14.ps; 49:16; 73:26. By His Resurrection from the Dead, Jesus proved that everlasting life was real.

41
Does the Bible Indicate that God is Freedom"?

Yes. The Book of Exodus states that God, through Moses, led the early Hebrews out of slavery in Egypt to Freedom in the "Promised Land", though Moses did not reach the "Promised Land" himself due to his death.

Also, Freedom from the bondage of sin and its punishment was exemplified by Jesus, who assured pardon of all sins. "All have sinned and are deprived of the glory of God. They are justified freely by His grace through the redemption in Jesus Christ, whom God set forth as an expiation of sins previously committed." Rom 3:23-25. God is Freedom.

42
Does Stress in our Lives have Value?

While a student at the College of St. Thomas in St. Paul, I wrote a paper entitled "Stress is Good" for a class called "English Composition", through an exchange program at St. Catherine's College. Looking back on that paper, I must qualify that statement with the notion that a "certain amount of stress" is good, which I actually meant to say in that paper. Stress can increase our challenge to perform, which can help motivate us to perform better. When encountering stress, we are "tested" to become better. In writing my books I have encountered stress, but manageable stress, which I humbly believe improved my writing.

When tested by stress we show our "true colors". By meeting stress and conquering it, we come out stronger and achieve more. Stress is not necessarily our enemy, but we should not seek out stress unless we believe we can conquer it—something that is difficult to know, at times. This is in line with setting reasonable goals in our lives.

However, we should not arbitrarily set limits on what we can achieve, but trust God if we have set a "high bar" for ourselves. God's Love can help us, for God is Love, Happiness and Freedom.

43
"I Did it My Way"

The title of the song above presents an interesting view of life to me. "Doing it my way" did not always work out well for me or for others I affected. I do have regrets.

However, I have no regrets or complaints concerning Divine Providence (What God has given me). But, some of my selfish desires and actions with others have not led me, or others I affected, directly to Happiness.

In particular, when engaged to my wife, I asked her to walk through a foot of snow for one-half mile to ice fish, catching only a few small perch. On another occasion, I asked her to fish when the temperature was 6 degrees to catch only a few crappies. Finally the worst and most "unjust test" I put to my future wife was when fishing in my boat in Canada. It was a sunny day in June and pleasant on the lake. However, she began to complain about sunburn on her hands. I did not pay that much attention, because I was not experiencing sunburn. Also, I did not know that a prescription drug she was taking caused sunburn. So, I kept saying to her "just one more cast" as I often did, and we kept fishing. One more cast turned into several. Finally, when she put her hands in the water to cool them off, and started crying, I decided that it was time to go to shore—something long overdue. Kathy certainly passed my "unjust tests" of love for me and she had the courage to marry me despite those "unjust tests". I thanked her for her love and courage later in our marriage and still do today in prayer and with the dedication of this book to her.

In conclusion, "doing it my way" was not always the "best" way. We should try to do it God's way, even if that means "getting on our knees". (I finding "timing" in my life again, as the song 'On My Knees" sung by Charlie Rich and Janie Fricke and written by Charlie Rich played on my phone when ending this article, just AFTER writing "getting on our knees". I did not plan that. It just happened.)

44
Christ's "New Way": Forgiveness

Before Jesus, I have said there was forgiveness, but it was not as prevalent as after Jesus. Revenge was considered justice in the Old Testament: "An eye for an eye and a tooth for a tooth". Jesus's commandment to "forgive our brother 70 times 7 times" was something new, I believe.

Since Jesus, I believe that forgiveness has become even more important. I have said that "without forgiveness, there is no hope for the sinner". (article 79, God is Love). We are all sinners, so there is little hope for mankind without forgiveness. This pertains to domestic as well as international relationships.

Jesus started the movement towards forgiveness over two thousand years ago. Today, let's continue it and expand it to bring and maintain Peace and Freedom. God is Peace and Freedom.

45
Do We "Write People Off" as Unforgivable?

At times, some of us are judgmental and do not forgive others as commanded by Jesus. However, there is no limit to God's Love and Forgiveness. We are limited, but if God does not "write people off", why should we do it?

If we love everyone as Jesus commanded, we will forgive them. Forgiveness, based on Love and the Truth, is the cement that holds societies together. God is Love and Freedom.

46
God and Freedom

"The more you are led by God's Love, the more you become yourself and it is all done without ever losing your freedom.... God made a world in which a man and a woman would rise to moral heights, not by that blind driving power which makes the sun rise each morning, but rather by the exercise of that freedom in which one may fight the good fight and enjoy the reward of victory—for no one shall be crowned unless he has struggled." (from the Wisdom of Fulton Sheen with introduction by Matthew Kelley and published by Blue Sparrow, p. 34)

47
Optimism: Does it Cause False Hope?

Optimism is defined in the dictionary (Funk and Wagnalls) as "a disposition to look on the bright side of things". Based on that definition, optimism does NOT necessarily cause false hope. We should try to understand a situation which may look "dire" or very bad, but we can still look for a "silver lining in the cloud".

Optimism is related to trust in God. If we look on the "bright side" based on trust in God, we will be much happier. Pessimism, on the other hand, can lead to despair and much unhappiness, possibly over something that currently is not really that bad and may not even become something very bad.

To maintain happiness and freedom is our lives, we should not succumb to pessimism, but practice optimism. This is not to say we should not intelligently realize a bad situation and try to improve it, but also realize that our faith and trust in God CAN help us improve the situation. Then, we can enjoy God's Love and Protection with the Freedom that it brings. God is Freedom.

48
Who Crucified Christ and for What Reasons?

Jesus was very popular with the masses of people after performing miracles and preaching (i.e., Multiplying the fishes; the Sermon on the Mount with the Beatitudes). Influential Jewish leaders were afraid of His power and influence over the people. So much that Caiaphas, a high priest, counseled the Jews that "better that one man should die than the people". John 18:14

Caiaphas was afraid that Jesus might cause an insurrection.

Jesus probably knew he could raise an insurrection to try to defend Himself. But, He also knew it was His fate to die— "drink of the cup" His Father gave Him.

Pilate received Jesus from the Jewish chief priests and elders, who wanted Pilate to crucify Him. When the crowd, which had gathered kept chanting: "crucify Him, crucify Him", Pilate asked: "Why, what has He done?" This got no answer from the crowd of Jews except to chant louder to crucify Jesus. Matt 27:22. After repeatedly trying to release Jesus, Pilate saw that it was to no avail, so he had him crucified, fearing a riot from the angry mob. Pilate "washed his hands" of responsibility for Christ's crucifixion after finding no guilt in Jesus, so he blamed the Jews.

Jesus had said to Pilate: "You have no power over me if it had not been given to you from above. For this reason, the one who handed me over to you has the greater sin." John 19:11 This accusation could fit either Judas or Caiaphas as the one who "has the greater sin". Judas handed Jesus over to Caiaphas. Caiaphas hoped that Pilate would order Jesus to be crucified. Judas probably did not know that he set Jesus up for crucifixion when handing him over to the Jewish leaders. He probably did it to please the Jewish leaders

(Caiaphas and others) and receive money from them for doing so. He realized his guilt when learning of Christ being condemned to death. "Then, Judas, his betrayer, seeing, that Jesus had been condemned, deeply regretted what he had done. He returned the thirty pieces of silver to the chief priests and elders, saying, "I have sinned in betraying innocent blood". They said "What is that to us. Look to it yourself". Flinging the money into the temple, he departed and went off and hanged himself." Matt 27: 3-5. It is not known whether God forgave Judas of such serious sins of betrayal and despair. I believe many assume God did not forgive him, but we really do not know. However, according to Scripture, Jesus said to His apostles the night before He was crucified: "Woe to that man by whom the Son of Man is betrayed. It would be better for that man if he had never been born." Mark 14:21

In conclusion, Jesus did not plan an insurrection, but was like a "lamb led to the slaughter". He did not fight back. But, His reward for dying for mankind was His Resurrection. We today inherit Christ's promise of Everlasting Life, which can begin as Happiness in this lifetime. Just as Jesus freely accepted His fate, so are we free to accept or reject God's will in our lives. God is Freedom.

49
Work and our Goals

When work runs counter to our goals in life, perhaps we are doing the wrong type of work or the right work in the wrong way. Or perhaps, we have set the wrong goals in life, and should reset them to match our work.

Perhaps, we should reset our primary goal to become attaining Heaven through Love of God and Love of Others as Ourselves. Then perform work that matches that goal. We should ask the Holy Spirit to guide us in that work.

50
Planting "Good Seeds" to Produce "Good Fruits"

Scripture says that if "good seed" falls on "rich soil", it will produce "good fruit". Matt 13:23

"Good seed" is the word of God. "Good fruit" are good works with all its benefits. "Rich soil" refers to "the one who hears the word (of God) and understands it" and keeps it.

If you, the reader, are "rich soil", you will produce "good fruit". I humbly hope that my books help to enrich your "soil" by "opening you up to the Holy Spirit "to better understand God's message in the Bible ("good seed") and help to bring you more Freedom, so that you can produce "good fruit" by better serving God and others. God is Freedom!

God Love and Bless You!

Michael John DeNucci lives in Cumberland, WI and is a freelance writer for God and Mankind.

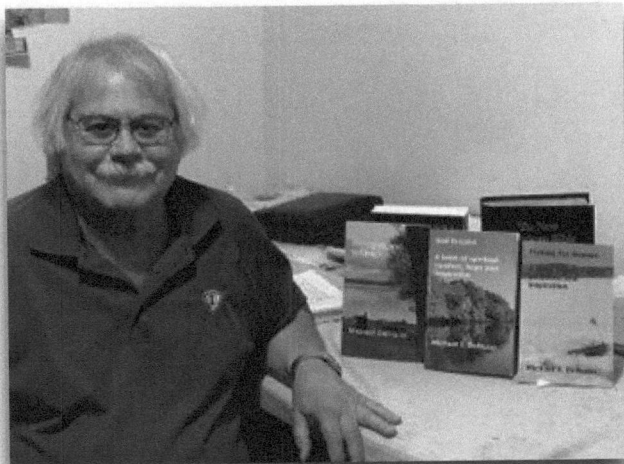

Michael John DeNucci attended his first two years of high school at Holy Cross Seminary in Lacrosse, Wisconsin and then returned to graduate from Cumberland High School. He went on to earn his Bachelor's Degree in Political Science from the College of St Thomas in St Paul, Minnesota, attended the University of Wisconsin at Madison partially completing an MBA, and then earning a Master's Degree in Industrial Relations from the University of Minnesota. He is an Army Veteran who has served stateside and in Germany. He has held a variety of jobs over his lifetime which have broadened his perspectives on the relationship of God and Mankind.

Other Books by Michael John DeNucci

"Thoughts and Writings"

"Fishing for Heaven?"

"God is Love"

"Is God Happiness?"

"Is Love the Truth?"

"Happiness is the Truth"

"God Is the Truth"

"Is Love Freedom?"

"Is God Mercy?"

"Is God Peace?"